D1111253

Soccer

GAME
INTELLIGENCE

The Difference-Maker in Officiating

IQ

Edited By Carl P. Schwartz
and Dan C. Heldman

FROM *REFEREE* MAGAZINE & THE NATIONAL ASSOCIATION OF SPORTS OFFICIALS

Soccer Game Intelligence: The Difference-Maker in Officiating

Edited by Carl P. Schwartz and Dan C. Heldman

Cover and layout by Matt Bowen, graphic designer, *Referee* magazine

Published by Referee Enterprises, Inc., and the National Association of Sports Officials.

Printed in the United States of America

ISBN-13: 978-1-58208-162-5

TABLE OF CONTENTS

INTRODUCTION

The successful official (certainly the wise one) accepts the rules and mechanics changes over the years and adapts to them. The only way to stay on top of things is to improve one's game intelligence. That's what this book aims to do.

Trying to cull game intelligence from a decade of soccer articles in *Referee* was an amazing journey. This compilation of articles we selected will expose you to many topics that are important both within and outside the lines of a soccer field. Personality, assessments, field size, safety, consistency and more are addressed. The chapters delve deep into a topic, break it down and provide examples to make a teaching point. Each chapter contains "Top Takeaways," written by us as the editors, that give guidance for new and advanced referees.

A number of skilled writers and talented officials contributed to this book. All the material was previously published in *Referee*. In some cases it was edited for space and connectivity. You will read the words of the late Pat Smith, former National Director of Assessment and Eddie Pearson award winner; Todd Abraham, NISOA National Director of Instruction; Gil Weber, National Referee Emeritus and frequent author of USSF publications; Doug Smith, frequent *Referee* contributor and former State Director of Instruction; Bob Wertz, former chair of the U.S. Youth Soccer Referee Committee and accredited ontological coach; Jeffrey Caminsky, author of *The Referee's Survival Guide: Practical Suggestions for Soccer Officials*; Josef Zeevi, former State Referee and co-author of *Guide for Fourth Officials*; veteran referee Vince DeFranco; and USSF instructor Conor McGahey. Their *Referee* contributions, along with several magazine articles we wrote, led to the creation of this book.

Here's hoping this book takes your game intelligence to new heights.

Carl P. Schwartz
Referee Soccer Coordinator
Former National Assessor

Dan C. Heldman
Referee Editorial Contributor
National Instructor Trainer

CHAPTER

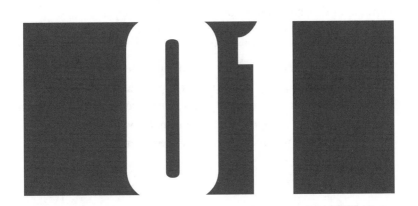

01

GO BEYOND
THE BASICS

The late Ken Aston was recognized throughout the world as one of the foremost authorities on soccer officiating procedures and management. He published an incisive article entitled "Sink or Swim," which evoked latent thoughts and feelings: How should we share our knowledge and experience of practical application under critical conditions of stress and emotion?

That is the moment when the cold print of the *Laws of the Game* (or rulebooks) is simply not enough to get an inexperienced referee successfully, or at least acceptably, through a moment of high anxiety. Here are a few reflections with the hope that you may share in the experience and wisdom of Aston.

LOOK BEHIND THE LAWS

Imagine a person joining the police force as a trainee. The individual learns the laws of his or her game: criminal law, civil law, power of search, power of arrest and so on. At the end of the course, he or she is tested on what was taught. Equally important, the individual learns how to deal with the public. In other words, the trainee learns people management and public relations skills. Then if the trainee satisfies his or her superiors, the trainee enters a probationary period under the supervision of experienced police officers.

Is it possible for referees to learn from that method of training? Yes, and you should do so immediately. In many cases, entry-level referees learn the 17 Laws and are coached through taking the written test, but they often do not actually learn how to referee.

A case in point: Students learn the reasons for giving yellow or red cards, but many are not taught the mechanics of giving a card. Many instructors never ask students to role-play what to say to the player or what questions to ask: the details of number, name (and first initial), why the player is being cautioned or red-carded and what happens in the event of repetition of unfavorable conduct. Instructors should demonstrate the body language, position relative to the field of play and position relative to the player. Referees who thrust a card in the player's face often do not realize that should not be done.

Not role-playing is tantamount to teaching swimming in a classroom setting giving instruction on breaststroke, backstroke, sidestroke or crawl but never going into the water. When the instructor finally casts the students into the deep end of the pool, telling them, "Sink or swim," a few swim but many climb out, never to be seen near the pool again. Does that sound familiar?

The question arises: How many young referees are actually taught how to referee?

Soccer administrators should not dwell on what referees do wrong, but rather emphasize how to do it right. As an example, Law 11, offside, has been drummed into the head of every referee. Most referees in the country truly understand Law 11. Mistakes arise through lack of concentration, not lack of knowledge. Lack of concentration is usually caused by "ball watching." We don't need to beat experienced referees to death with Law 11.

When thinking in terms of coaches, the picture is very different; the perception has altered. Many coaches do not, cannot or will not understand the concept of the offside law. The terms "passive," "active," "gaining an advantage" and "interfering with" are foreign to many coaches. They believe that the position, not the intent, is paramount.

IMPLEMENT HANDS-ON TRAINING

What should we teach? How many instructors learned to teach with a hands-on approach? That is not meant as a criticism of instructors who have only rules knowledge, but you must employ every available instructional aid to illustrate the point, especially when less-experienced referees have not actually played the game. New referees must experience the "other side of the coin." Teach with a hands-on approach — role-plays, drills, simulations — to get the students involved.

1. Dissent.
We must teach recognition of dissent and how to deal with it (especially how to differentiate between emotional dissent and the more critical, calculated type). We must teach anticipation by reading body language. We must teach how to look into a player's eyes and know that player is going to jump into a goalkeeper, not try to head the ball.

2. Language.
We must discuss offensive, insulting or abusive language and what the Law requires referees to do about it. There should be no quarter given by instructors teaching that subject and none given by referees enforcing the Law. We must teach the correct mechanics of giving a sanction card to a player, rather than a simple, cursory gesture given in a demeaning manner.

3. Injuries.
Dealing with injuries, real and imagined, requires attention. Abusive coaches must be dealt with, regardless of reputation.

4. Advantage.
The use and misuse of the advantage clause is a prominent subject. Emphasize common sense, good judgment and courage. Poor excuses are not acceptable.

5. Arm signals, whistles and flags.
If they're worth doing, then they're worth doing properly. Instructors should schedule time for everyone to participate in vital practice sessions.

6. Positioning.
The art of being where you should be, when you should be there must be emphasized. That goes for the officials on the touchline as well as for the referee.

7. Partners.
Model how to work with club linespeople so that they know the limits of their duties. Role-play a discussion with assistant referees and fourth officials. Show newer referees how to establish camaraderie, cooperation and communication.

8. Walls.
Wall management is often approached in a lackadaisical manner due to a lack of emphasis on discipline, distance, mechanics and ball aerodynamics. Substantial emphasis for recertifying referees is needed. The eventual goal is perfection and that requires much hands-on demonstration.

9. Gamesmanship.
Teaching by demonstrating and emphasizing the differences between gamesmanship and unsporting behavior is needed to apply the Law and to control the game to the satisfaction and enjoyment of all concerned. There are many other practical matters concerning techniques that can be demonstrated in our limited classroom hours.

KEEP UP WITH THE GAME

Without question, the game 60 years ago was a totally different one. The skill level today is much higher, the tempo is much faster and coaches orchestrate fouls for tactical and strategic advantage. Along with the positive changes in the game, a prevalent attitude now says that while winning is wonderful, losing is a cardinal sin.

Players do not have the discipline they used to have.

They do not accept decisions as readily. Dissent is not about freedom of speech, but about game control. Dissenting actions challenge the authority of the referee. Whereas 60 years ago "being booked" was an infrequent situation in the English First Division, it now occurs with substantially greater frequency. Players testing referees are determined to usurp their authority, and referees must learn the intricacies of people management to avoid being overrun by gamesmanship. Both individuals and groups will challenge onfield referees: Are the referees ready? Have instructors prepared referees for what they will face on the field?

On the positive side, coaches look to the referee to be decisive, strong, fair and approachable, but not fearful.

You must look emphatically toward new referees: give them encouragement, suggest methods of improvement, moderate minor shortcomings into revised positioning or mechanics and seek to better them in everyone's eyes.

To do so, teach by example. Demonstrate how to recognize problems and to deal with them, not with a textbook approach, but with "hands-on" application. Referees must show self-confidence, empathy and a facial expression that tells the

TOP TAKEAWAYS

New Referee: Get a mentor. Get someone with more knowledge about refereeing than you have and ask him or her for help. If you are a little fuzzy on Law 10, ask questions until you understand. If the concept of a trivial foul during U-14 play is the hardest thing you are dealing with, get that mentor to watch your game and discuss what contact you whistled versus what could let go.

Experienced Referee: Get a mentor and be a mentor. Use film study, attend training sessions and get some of the older books (Robert Evans and Edward Bellion's For the Good of the Game, Eric Sellin's The Inner Game of Soccer or Stanley Lover's Association Football Match Control). Learn from the early masters and then be ready to pass those lessons along to those following your footsteps.

players, "I am enjoying the game with you." By showing younger referees the alternatives and teaching them the right things to say, you will be well on the way to putting less-experienced referees on the road to enjoyment, pride and success.

FULFILL YOUR SPECIAL DUTY

Referees are not special people doing an ordinary job, but ordinary people doing a special job.

It may be that our present system dwells too much on test-taking and not enough on making good referees. With the best of intentions, there are instructors who tell students what needs to be done. That, in itself, is not bad. But it must be followed up with several practical sessions. The referee-in-training needs to stand up and do something to incorporate the knowledge. Veteran instructors will ensure their students not only know what the Laws say, but also understand when and how to use that knowledge.

CHAPTER

02

IS THE FIELD
SAFE FOR PLAY?

It's Sunday morning. You wake up to head out to referee after a long night of steady rainfall, followed by a strong cold front coming through. It's happened to most officials. You may think to yourself, "Do I really have to referee in *this* weather?" You get in your vehicle, drive to the complex and upon going out to the field, you come across a surface that has you scratching your head, saying to yourself, "I can't believe the owner of this field hasn't closed it."

If you're doing mostly travel games or higher level competition, teams have traveled a good distance to get to the game. They stand to be put at considerable expense both in time and money should the game get cancelled due to poor field conditions. Regardless of the level, you must make a fair and accurate decision regarding a cancellation, for the safety and enjoyment of the participants.

WET FIELD

On wet playing surfaces, it is imperative that players have enough traction so that when they make a cut, they don't slip and fall. When fields are muddy, not only should the players be wearing longer studs, so should the referee. If you cannot jog around the field to warm up without slipping, then how are the players going to be able to move safely at game time?

On pitches that are in poorer-than-average shape, you will find a good amount of standing water. Puddles are not reason alone to abandon a match; however, location and size of puddles can affect your decision. If players cannot predict when they will be able to stop and plant their feet, they might pull muscles and twist ankles, which is probably not the safest field for them to be playing on. Standing water in one or both goal-mouths affects fairness. Abandonment should be a consideration. Water that has drained to the field edges might be a minor consideration.

Anthony Vasoli, FIFA assistant referee, who frequently works top-level professional games in the U.S., says, "In order to determine if a drenched field of play is acceptable and safe, the following method works quite well: Take a soccer ball and drop it to the ground from chest level on several locations on the field of play. If the ball does not bounce back up at all — merely 'splashing down' or worse, floating — at several locations on the field, the field is probably too wet to play on safely."

Keep your assistants in mind too — that is one reason to practice using the right-wing/left-back diagonal system. Since your assistants cannot vary their position like the referee can, you should be well-versed in how to operate effectively in a "reverse" diagonal, so they don't have to slog through the mud of the previous game.

HOT WEATHER

Competition authorities below the professional levels may dictate mandatory water breaks in hot weather or they may shorten halves or take similar measures. What if no such authority exists? Use common sense — give players and your referee team the necessary means to hydrate. Don't forget to add time or stop the clock. Many leagues make those judgments based on a heat index chart (combination of temperature and humidity), which is available at www.weather.com.

COLD WEATHER

When the weather is cold, how cold is too cold? Obviously if it is snowing and you can no longer see the markings, abandon. In general, games are played in the cold, but if the participants can no longer feel body parts, it's time to abandon. Many leagues consult a wind chill index (combination of outside temperature and wind). Visit www.weather.com for an example.

WIND

Referees need to keep a few things in mind on windy days. As always, make certain portable goals are anchored securely. Second, can a free kick be taken without the ball rolling with the wind? If that cannot happen (or you can't devise a workaround like tiny piles of sand), the game needs to be abandoned. In some windy areas, leagues have a "ball holder" rule. If the ball will not stay stationary for a dead ball kick, they allow a ball holder to place one finger on the ball.

DUSK/FOG

If you have a match scheduled without lights, check what time sunset is before you leave. Considering clouds, matches can typically be played from 10-30 minutes after sunset before you will need to abandon. Knowing that before the game, and knowing that the game could not play full halves, discuss with team managers your decision to shorten the halves to get the game in two equal-length halves. If you must abandon the match due to insufficient daylight, include those details in the match report (time in game of abandonment, score at the time, etc.).

TOP TAKEAWAYS

New Referee: You are going to have to make decisions about what to do in poor weather and sloppy field conditions. Do what your local league calls for. Ask your mentor, instructor or clinician. Use the chapter's guidelines as well.

Experienced Referee: You've got the same decisions to make in regard to weather, but there will be more pressure. The teams will have traveled from farther away. Instead of 20 fans surrounding the field, a crowd of 2,000 paid fans may already be seated. Safety comes first. Get information — weather bureau, local TV forecasters, site administrators, availability of other fields — then make a decision. Expect at least one party to be very upset with your decision.

If you can't tell the color difference between the teams' jerseys from halfway across the field (even though you won't be judging play from there), then the conditions are not adequate for the match to continue. Consider what type of sightlines your assistants have to put up with when making your decision.

CHAPTER

03

UNDER THE LIGHTS

There is something better about a game played under the lights. Millions of people enjoy a soccer game no matter where it's played or who the contestants are. Envision the excitement of a stadium filled with roaring fans as the players ply their trade under the lights.

Many officials get the joy of refereeing contests under the lights. At all levels, there are differences that you want to be aware of as you embark on such a game.

PRESSURE AT NIGHT

In general, games played under the lights have a higher level of competition — perhaps schools that are intense rivals or part of a homecoming weekend. Athletic directors are likely to showcase matches involving top teams: big matches, high levels of play.

Associated with the high level of play comes a larger viewing base. Many loyal fans will make the playoff games no matter when they take place. Fiscal realities dictate that many parents and neighbors have to work during the day. But they can often make an evening game.

A highly competitive match in front of a lot of fans adds up to pressure. Pressure on the players and coaching staffs add up to pressure on the officiating team.

Players used to playing in front of 60 to 100 fans suddenly find themselves in front of a lot more. That's intimidating. Some will react well. Some will overreact and cause discipline problems for the referees.

Coaches might feel the heat a little — the need to win at district and advance to sectionals. Maybe the press reminded them of last year's disappointing loss. Wrapped a little tighter than normal, the coaches may feel the need to express their frustrations in an uncharacteristic manner. Are you ready?

OTHER GAME PERSONNEL

At the professional level, there are team liaisons and stadium representatives performing their jobs proficiently. Those you encounter might not have the same degree of expertise.

Does the custodian know to let you into your dressing rooms? Perhaps since it is now a night game, the normal table personnel aren't available and stand-ins are filling the assignments. Referees, are you ready for that?

You'll also get extra help that might not be available during a daylight contest. There is liable to be a school representative. There is likely to be security. Do they know your needs? Do you know theirs?

THE REFEREE

Are you ready? You've been assigned a game. You've been there a dozen times for day games, but do you know the field location for the evening game? Do you know where to park (particularly with many more people there)? Does your whole crew have that information? Including the fourth official (yes, you may now have a fourth official)? Have you reviewed guidelines for the fourth official's duties?

SCOUT IT OUT

Since it is a new setting, gather as much information as you can. If you know playoff games are held in Memorial Stadium, go to a game played there at night, perhaps even a football game. See the differences. Ask security if you can get to field level. Use halftime to walk all areas of the park.

GAME-DAY PREPARATION

Normally, you eat a hearty breakfast, a lunch to prepare your body for the afternoon's activities and eat dinner after the game. Now you have to factor in when to eat dinner. You can't go without any food from noon until the final whistle — that nutritional deprivation would hurt your concentration and performance. You are not used to eating a light early evening meal just prior to strenuous physical activity. Practice a few times during your training runs.

Your kit is packed and ready for a typical day game. You rush through light traffic to the field and start the game. But now you've got time. Too often, referees working their first evening games make wrong decisions. Rather than scurry home through rush-hour traffic, why not use that time to calm yourself? Find a park near the stadium. Relax. Invite your officiating team to share a light meal with you.

ASSISTANT REFEREES

If you have bright or fluorescent flags, bring them out. Check your running path. If you are on a football field, there are liable to be sprinkler heads in your path. Know that before you get there at a full sprint. Depth perception is going to present difficulty on some decisions.

The fourth official may need an extra layer of clothing.

Tarek Kahn, an emeritus National Referee, says, "The intra-referee signals that work during the day may need to be modified (time left and other 'silent' signals). Work that out

---

TOP TAKEAWAYS

New Referee: You'll probably be working as an assistant or fourth official for your first night game. The tips in this chapter still apply to you: eating patterns, vision, pressure. Knowing about those aspects ahead of time might help you. Ask questions of your referee.

Experienced Referee: Hopefully you've already worked a night game or two and have learned a few lessons. Trying to get the rest of the crew ready for the game will be one of your tougher challenges. Enjoy the higher level of play!

in pregame as you walk the field. Work out your 'missed flag' mechanics, as that is more likely during an evening contest."

VISION

It's still a soccer game. The assigner had enough faith in you to assign you to the game. You've done it hundreds of times. But there is one difference.

Your eyes react differently under the artificial light. Distance vision is not as distinct, so you'll need to work slightly closer to play than normal. Balance that with not getting in the way. And you may have considerably more difficulty reading your watch or notebook, particularly if you normally wear reading glasses but are refereeing the contest without your contacts or glasses.

Inevitably, there are shadows or dark spots on the fields. That's why you did your scouting trip days before your game. Know where those spots are and anticipate as play heads into those areas.

You cannot change the physiology of your vision, but you can get used to some aspects of it. Through a process called acculturation, if you place yourself in the setting often enough, you start to get used to the night-reduced accuracy of vision. Plan family walks after dinner. Place yourself in the setting.

Try not to look directly into the light standards. The brief flash of intense light will affect your retinas, causing "after images" (spots in front of your eyes), and diminishing your acuity until your eyes readjust. One veteran referee said, "The lights will teach in an unforgiving manner that it's unnecessary to follow the ball above head height. Do not visually follow air balls."

BIG NIGHT

First, congratulations on being selected to work the game. There will be some added stress and pressure. Get a full evening's rest the night before. Your physical and mental preparations will yield dividends.

Remember to use the able assistance of those around you — administrators, table officials and officiating partners. Smile. Enjoy the game.

CHAPTER

04

WHEN THEY'RE WATCHING YOU

You may profess that being assessed doesn't change your style, but there are far too many people who offer their own stories about referees who change when an assessor shows up for an upgrade assessment with a clipboard and a folding chair. Players, coaches and fans attest to that "fact" as well.

Assessments should change you, but only for those games after you've gotten feedback and constructive criticism.

OVER-OFFICIATE

The most notable change when a referee is assessed is that the referee tends to over-officiate the contest. There is no concrete definition for that term, but basically the referee calls an extra five or six fouls each half, enough to dampen some of the exciting physical play that typically accompanies highly skilled players on a high-level stage. Referees are showing the assessor they can control a match, but they destroy its flow. Substitutions are more "by the book." There might be an unexpected penalty kick.

CARD USAGE

Referees tend to not use their misconduct cards in the same manner when being assessed as they do in a regular game. They tend to not use a needed card to show the assessor they have the skills to get through the contest without resorting to cards. Or they pop one or two quick cards early in the game and then run into problems when a player with a "light" card commits a further action that should result in a card. There is nowhere to hide on that one.

RUNNING PATTERNS

Showing off, the referees run farther, deeper and wider than they normally do. As a result, they are seeing contact situations from different angles than normal. That affects their judgment on contact situations and results in awkward moments while the referees try to interpret that data from that new angle and distance. Their confidence is shaken. And they run out of gas in the late stages of a contest.

Some well-respected assessors contributed their thoughts on assessments and what referees should and shouldn't do when being assessed.

THINKING

"The worst thing that a referee can do when being assessed is to think, 'What would this assessor do in a particular situation?' or 'Is this how the assessor would call this match? Then I must call it in the same manner in order to pass,'" said Austin Gomez, a National Assessor from St. Louis. "That line of reasoning is horrible! The most important concept for the referee is to be yourself! If you make mistakes, so be it — that is the human element, which will always be involved in every soccer game. Learn from the mistake."

EGO

"Another factor involved in assessment is the matter of referee egotism," said Robert Sumpter, NISOA Honor Award winner, former National Referee and current National Assessor. "Many referees are of the attitude that they only want to hear an assessor say that their performance is good or great. As a result, referees will try to make sure they perform in that particular game so that the assessor will only have good things to report. I believe that referee egotism is a characteristic not unfamiliar among referees."

SIGNALS/POSITIONING

"Referees realize they must be formal with their signals and positioning — thus they begin to lose sight of their first job, which is making sure players have a safe environment to play in," said Kim Vieira, National Referee, NISOA Regional representative and inductee into the NISOA Hall of Fame. "They become so concerned with 'looking good and using proper mechanics' that they take themselves totally out of the play. Players begin to realize that and may get out of hand. Officials being assessed must control and conduct themselves as though the assessor is not there."

FEEDBACK

The most important aspect of having an assessor is to get positive and constructive feedback as to how the official conducted the game. That is not the time to get into a verbal confrontation with the assessor. Assessors, for the most part, have committed their time and expenses to be there for the assessment, so take the comments from a point of view that the assessor is trying to help your career, not hinder it.

"For those referees who react (by changing the way they referee), those assessments mean less than they should," said Sumpter, "because the results are false, and cannot possibly

---

TOP TAKEAWAYS

New Referee: For some, assessments are shrouded in mystery — many feel scared or intimidated. Don't be concerned. Learn from assessments and improve as a result of them.

Experienced Referee: The point of an assessment is to change your style (if needed), just not on the match being assessed. So, for the game you are being assessed on, just work in the manner that got you that assignment. Do what you do best. If improvements are needed, they'll be pointed out.

help the referee being assessed as much as if they had been able to perform at their normal level."

Avoid the pitfalls that many referees experience when being assessed. Referee like you would without the assessment. Positive change comes afterward.

CHAPTER

05

WALK PERSONALITY, TALK PERSONALITY

Do you have a winning personality? If you have all the other skills of a great official, does it matter how you come across to others on the field?

Many factors go into improving your refereeing. You need to know the rules. As a result, you need to hit the books or have rules discussions with instructors and fellow referees. And you need to understand how to implement the rules. You know, "What if it's Thursday and a player from a visiting team on a field that is small (but approved by prior written consent) has a cast on her wrist? ..." That's just one of a variety of scenarios that could happen in your match. Whatever your level, you need to have the rules discussions and work through the plays.

You must also have good foul recognition and the ability to adjust to varying levels of play. That means all kinds of refereeing. Work the "easy" games, the "hard" games, the games with teams of different skills, backgrounds, styles of play, and hopefully you will have someone there to watch and provide feedback about your performance.

What about fitness? Go off to the track for training and improvement. Run laps, laps and more laps for endurance and cardio and then do sprints for speed and strength improvements until you drop. Run up and down hills, too.

Those are necessary steps in becoming better, but there is still that one factor that most referees fail to consider: their personality. Yes, we're all angels, and the best at everything we try. We never have bad days. Cough. However difficult, our personality is one of those things that each of us should understand about ourselves in order to become better.

It's not necessary to relay how we may have gotten our personalities and what some of the basic tools of psychoanalysis might yield. But we can look at a few personality factors: how we present ourselves to players, coaches and other officials, and how to use personality effectively to help manage players.

PERSONALITY CLOSE-UP

One referee is often described as bright, friendly, very rules-knowledgeable, extremely ethical but also somewhat inflexible and, at times, a slave to the rules. Fellow officials enjoy his company, but his humor occasionally causes slight tension. Assigners will put him on just about any game but it took a long time for him to get there. After years of not understanding why things weren't moving along as rapidly as he'd like, that referee (call him Bob) had a chance to talk with a referee he'd known for years (Tom) — one he respected and with whom he had an open relationship. The talk was difficult, but eye-opening.

Bob asked Tom for thoughts on why Bob's refereeing seemed to have reached a plateau. Tom indicated that Bob's strong moral position about right and wrong may be a factor. Tom gave an example: When you referee, and you see B7 wearing jewelry, you ask B7 to take it off. Bob replied, "Of course, it's in the rules and it certainly makes sense from a safety point of view." Tom inquired about how that conversation goes. Bob said, "I simply asked B7 to remove the jewelry, since the rules didn't allow it." Tom responded: "Ah, so one of the first contacts you have with B7 sets up a right-wrong rule presentation."

Tom continued, "So let's assume that five minutes into the game B7 gets fouled, but you allow play to continue as it's either trifling or you allow advantage. B7 comes back to you, telling you to call those things!"

"But Tom," said Bob, "there's no point in calling those little things. You know that!"

"Yes, I do," said Tom, "but because you set out a fairly black-and-white rule situation before the game, it's likely B7 figured you were going to be fairly straight up and down about what is or isn't a foul."

Bob had a revelation. Maybe he was setting himself up to fail during the game by the way he dealt with things that came up before the game. He spent time figuring out different ways to handle the "black-and-white" issues and came up with a way to soften his pregame approach.

Tom pointed out that Bob had developed a very sharp wit that often worked against him. Not everyone responds well to sarcasm, said Tom. You're in your late 30s, so it's going to be hard for you to change your basic personality. Your strong drive to distinguish between right and wrong and habit of finding humor in every situation may be two factors that limit how you manage players and coaches. It's obvious that you are intelligent and compassionate, but sometimes (in the soccer environment) that doesn't come across. You see yourself as the arbitrator on the field but don't always concern yourself with the other participants.

TOUGH MESSAGE

Ultimately, Bob was able to wrap his head around it and make the connection between his refereeing skills (very high) and his refereeing personality (not suited for all situations). That's when it occurred to him that he might

ASSESS YOUR PERSONALITY

Do you have some personality quirks that have caused you problems during the season? As you enter the playoffs, are there some things you would like to change as the stakes grow higher? Are you finding yourself less tolerant of dissent than in the past — with a rising number of yellow cards for dissent? Have job stress and financial worries crept into your officiating?

The reverse may be true as well. You find a growing tolerance for actions that call for discipline. Are you still zero-tolerance for language (NFHS and NCAA)? Are you in step with the leadership's request to stomp out elbows contacting opponents above the shoulders? If you've been averaging 1.5 cards per game over your decade-long career, why have you suddenly only given five cards all season?

Outside Sources

If you've run through that laundry list of questions and all seems well, double check your thinking. Your mentor is perhaps your first stop. Ask your mentor to watch you for at least a half; see if your perception that all is well matches his or her impression. There is undoubtedly a fellow referee that you've worked with once or twice a season — either on his or her line or you've had him or her as your assistant a few times. If you've got a game together, ask that official if all appears well. And use the feedback you receive.

not have the right stuff to move as high up the ladder as he wished. And, over time, he developed new ways to deal with players, coaches and peers that allowed him to be better received as a referee.

There are a lot of ways to measure personality. One that is often used combines one of the following out of each category: introverted or extroverted; sensing (observing) or intuitive (instinctive); thinking or feeling; and judging or perceiving. So it's possible to be an extroverted, sensing, thinking, judging individual like Bob, or you could be some other combination of traits. You are you. Being aware of what you are allows you to moderate your behavior and presentation in useful ways, paying attention to how those qualities impact refereeing.

In Bob's case, there was a tough sense of right and wrong that was portrayed so strongly that the players expect a performance with no errors. They perceived that they had no room for errors from the referee. Maybe your personality is one of facilitation, which often comes

---

TOP TAKEAWAYS

New Referee: Everyone wants the big game right away. You are sure you've got all the needed tools to work that tournament final, the State Cup playoffs or the high school playoff game. While you may be fit, rules smart and work well with players, you've got to get a little "face time" around top coaches, assigners and other referees who regularly work at that level to be accepted into the newer heights that you aspire to. Without being showy or flashy, just work hard at things you do well and you'll be recognized. Conversations about you may be going on in the background. Some day you'll be tapped on the shoulder and asked to go see the assigner to get that big game.

Experienced Referee: You've worked for a decade to gain all the right skills, experience, fitness and rules knowledge. Hopefully, you've been a mentor and are starting to pass some of those lessons along to others. If you are this story's Bob, do you have a Tom you can talk to honestly? Do you see a lot of gray in your world black-and-white? Self-awareness is going to open a lot of doors for you.

across as weak and indecisive. Whatever it is, unless you are very young, it's going to be difficult to change. But knowing what your personality traits are will help you take important steps to improving your officiating (along with your knowledge, interpretation skills, foul recognition and — oh — fitness).

CHAPTER

06

WHISTLE WHILE
YOU WORK

Once the match begins, a referee's work starts in earnest. You earn every penny that the assignment is paying you. Referees run six miles or more during a competitive match, so you'll need every ounce of physical and mental stamina you can muster to communicate.

Because of its high pitch, shrill tone and ear-piercing decibel level, the whistle is the referee's most noticeable way of communicating. Many whistles are available, and the choice among them is entirely a matter of personal preference (unless the referee on the next field is using the same whistle — then one of you had better switch!).

RELAYING THE MESSAGE

Blowing the whistle communicates two possible messages: "Stop!" or "Start!" Regardless of context, that is the message you convey — simple, direct and unambiguous. Like Pavlov's dog, players quickly learn how to respond to your whistle. Depending on the circumstances, they know that they should either stop whatever they are doing or resume playing the game. But even something as simple as blowing a whistle can lead to complications.

MUSICIANSHIP

Most players and many spectators have met referees whose whistling technique leaves much to be desired. Rather than communicating decisiveness and resolve by a strong, confident blast, some sound more like a wheezing horse on its way to the glue factory. Most of those problems are easily corrected, and stem from improper technique — mostly from using the lips and throat to sound the whistle, rather than your diaphragm.

Musicians, especially singers and those who play wind instruments, quickly master the fundamentals of breath support. They know that without proper use of their diaphragm the tones they produce will be anemic. The diaphragm — the wall of muscle located under the front of the rib cage — is what musicians use to give power and substance to their sounds, and actors use to project their voices to the back of the theater. By supporting your tone with your diaphragm, which you do by breathing deeply and expanding your rib cage downward, you allow your entire torso to deliver air to your instrument, the whistle. The result is a stronger, more easily controlled sound for referee and musician alike.

Practice will have you sounding like the referee's equivalent of Pavarotti, able to split eardrums at will. That does not end the matter, for the whistle is more useful when used in a flexible, controlled manner to convey shadings of meaning beyond the simple commands of "stop" and "go."

TONE

Some referees use their whistle as if it were a fire alarm; others use it to talk to the players.

A fire alarm has one tone — loud — and one meaning: "Get out of here — now!" Some referees use their whistle in the same way. They have a single volume — loud if they feel confident, soft if they do not — which communicates nothing to the players beyond the two basic commands of "stop" and "go."

Veteran referees learn to vary the tone of their whistle and convey a wide range of sentiments and commands, each with a subtle shade of meaning. Some tones share information, some convey displeasure, some call down the Wrath of God from the heavens. As you might expect, the universal rule seems to be that the louder the whistle, the greater the referee's displeasure at whatever just happened. If you experiment with a variety of tones, you will hear the wide range of messages that are possible. With experience, you may come to appreciate the different meanings that you can convey, especially when combined with the appropriate body language or facial expression.

There is, of course, no secret code or intricate musical vocabulary to use. You just need to be aware that you can actually speak with your whistle, and then simply whistle whatever you mean.

TOP TAKEAWAYS

New Referee: You were probably introduced to the concept of "talking with the whistle" during your entry-level training. If that instantly made sense to you, good. Getting the correct message across is important.

Experienced Referee: Most referees do not use their whistle to its full effect. You can probably learn from others. If you are in an association or NISOA chapter, pick another referee whose whistle technique is better than yours and ask for some pointers.

CHAPTER

07

ADJUST TO THE SIZE

Except for young players who use "small sided" soccer rules, smaller fields (with smaller internal dimensions), smaller goals and smaller balls, the *Laws of the Game* provide a standard range of dimensions to which all matches must adhere.

There is a lot of leeway for individual fields to vary in size (100 to 130 yards, 50 to 100 yards, with international restrictions) while still being legal. It's clear that some referees fail to understand how putting big players (young adults and senior amateurs) on smaller fields impacts their officiating. All too often, referees come off the field following a game and wonder why they are told by assessors that their performance was less than stellar.

BIG PEOPLE ARE, WELL, BIGGER

Multiply that size difference by 23 (don't forget the referee!) and it becomes clear that more of the field space is being claimed by bodies — less field space for running, jumping, dribbling, etc. If you had to run to an airline's exit gate, would you rather run through an empty terminal or a crowded one? Wouldn't there be a greater likelihood of collisions and bumps in a crowded terminal?

Big people tend to take up disproportionately more space. Big people are usually older people who have been socialized into demanding and enforcing their "personal space" — that area immediately around the physical body within which the person becomes uncomfortable, if not aggressive, when intruded upon by another person. Of course, that space varies depending on how well the intruder is known (spouse, significant other, friend) and is highly correlated with the person's specific culture. It turns out that, holding culture constant, personal space expands as a person moves from childhood to adulthood. So, bigger people in a smaller field also means more intrusions into personal space.

Bigger people are also heavier, stronger and move faster. That means that the higher likelihood of contact or invasion of personal space translates into more consequential contact. With the potential of greater momentum involved, impacts are likely to be more serious — bigger people, more momentum in the collision; more momentum, greater likelihood of injury or an aggressive response. On the other hand, bigger people tend to be more sturdily constructed and may be able to shrug off contact easier, all other things being equal.

ELEMENTARY PHYSICS

First and most obviously, there is the higher incidence of contact. If players are bumping into each other more often, there may be more fouls, more opportunities to apply advantage, a greater need to distinguish between doubtful and felonious contact and a greater need to sort out improper contact that is trifling. In short, call sorting becomes a paramount issue. There is a greater need for the referee's intervention — talking, warning, calling advantage, whistling a stoppage — and the intervention needs to be more proactive to keep the match within reasonable bounds.

Crowding also tends to increase hard feelings. The frustration level is higher because, on a small field, collisions are harder to avoid. Add an enhanced level of frustration when the field is home to one team but not to the opponents. One team not accustomed to smaller dimensions translates into serious disadvantages in team strategies. Only one team will be able to make use of small-field strategies while the other will find itself constantly disadvantaged (at least for a while). Mistakes, miscues and misunderstandings will characterize the actions of one or both teams — at least in the early part of the match — until they figure things out.

With bigger people running around in a smaller space, the likelihood of the referee's (and the lead assistant's) line of sight being blocked increases greatly as well. Being near play becomes secondary to having a better angle. Simply put, there is a greater need to see what contact is occurring at the same time as the opportunities to get effective lines of sight are reduced. And the degree of eye contact and communication between the referee and each assistant rises in importance because seeing something that the other has missed is useless unless there are effective means of getting that information to the other official.

With so much field space taken up with big bodies, there is a significantly greater need for the referee to stay out of the way. That is the perfect time (because it is necessary, not just good procedure) to practice moving wide and deep. Passing lanes are more constricted and players need proportionately more of the available field to do their thing, leaving less for the referee. So, vow to get and stay outside of play. You should be doing that anyway, but with big people on a small field, it becomes a matter of survival.

Those are a few of the issues that affect your performance in a match played by big people on a small field. At the very least, however, you should be prepared to adjust your approach to a match (and discuss those adjustments in your pregame) when those game conditions arise.

TOP TAKEAWAYS

New Referee: You might not be able to deal with the emotions of big people on a little field, but you should recognize there will be more contact, more frustration, more fouls called. Your positioning will have to change — more across the field rather than up and down it. Some call that a wider diagonal.

Experienced Referee: With pregame awareness of what you're facing, your positioning should change to fit the game. Your call sorting will change from a "normal" game and you should have the experience to deal with the emotions and frustrations of the players, coaches and fans. Know that it's going to be exciting from the outset.

CHAPTER

08

THE HALFTIME BREAK

Every match, regardless of the rules under which it is played, includes a period of rest between the two equal periods of play (called variously the "midgame" or "halftime" break). Usually, referees don't pay much attention to that aspect of the game but there can be several important issues that arise in connection with the halftime break that you must be prepared to handle.

LENGTH

The break period can be up to 15 minutes long (FIFA) but the competition authority sets the specific number of minutes. It can be shortened, but only with the agreement of every player on both teams and the referee. Ironically, coaches do not have any say in that, though they are often the ones who may ask for it and who presume to "speak for" their team. You don't have to poll all the players to get their approval, but any player can assert his or her right to have the full midgame break as specified in the rules of competition. If someone does, the full break must be given.

NFHS allows shortening of the halftime break if both coaches agree. NCAA rules allow for shortening the break only to 10 or fewer minutes and requires only the agreement of the coaches.

The break period should not be shortened without a compelling reason (e.g., the possibility that the game would have to end prematurely due to a lack of light or to an approaching storm) and cannot be eliminated entirely. Remember, the officiating team also uses the break for its own purposes: players in a youth match get to come on and off the field but you are there the entire time. You also need the time to exchange information among officiating team members.

Most youth competitions allow for five minutes, NFHS rules specify 10 minutes (NCAA, 15 minutes). In order to keep a packed schedule of games running on time, you need to begin calling the teams out before the break is over because teams typically take at least a minute or two just to hear you, do their final gulps of water, have a moment of team-building cheers and then amble onto their half of the field. If you don't start bringing the teams on until the break period is actually over, your halftime break will actually be significantly longer and the schedule will suffer.

WHO IS A PLAYER?

Many referees unfortunately fail to consider that issue and, as a result, they will then not be prepared to handle correctly several issues that will be discussed in more detail. For now, however, note that every player leaving the field at the end of the first period of play remains a player of record during the halftime break.

For matches played in strict compliance with Law 3, it is not a difficult matter to manage because Law 3 requires you to know who those persons are anyway. The team's roster will have identified the 11 "starters" and both you and the bench-side assistant referee (and / or fourth official) will have adjusted the roster based on the relatively few (if any) substitutions that might have occurred during the first half.

In other words, you *always* know who is and who is not a player of record. That status carries over into and through the halftime break. If a team wants to substitute before beginning the second half, it must go through the formal substitution process outlined in Law 3, a process that must be completed before the whistle for the kick-off.

In youth play, where local rule exceptions allow for many substitutions to occur at specified times, with a full right of return, the only way to know who is a player of record during the halftime break is to know who was on the field when the whistle sounded to end the first half. As a practical matter, it may more easily be implemented by noting who was *not* on the field at the time — i.e., record who was on the bench when the half ended since that usually involves a much smaller group of persons.

A player of record who is only temporarily off the field at the end of the first half (to correct equipment or a bleeding problem, being treated for an injury, etc.) is still considered a player for purposes of the halftime break.

Everything noted applies equally to the period of rest between the end of the second half and any tie-breaking activities such as additional periods of play and/or kicks from the mark.

MISCONDUCT

As with any other stoppage of play, misconduct can occur during the halftime break. For cautions, no special issue arises, but a send off (red card) is different. FIFA and NCAA require that any player sent off during the halftime break cannot be replaced and the team therefore "plays down" when the second half begins. The NFHS rule is that a send-off issued during the halftime break is a "soft red" and the team does not play down even if the person sent off was a player of record at the time.

Accordingly, for a FIFA/NCAA match, you need to know whether the person whom you have just red carded is or is not a player because the consequences for the person's team are radically different based on the answer. Not surprisingly, *you* are the one who needs to know that, not the person just sent off nor the coach (each of whom has a vested interest in declaring that the person was not on the field at the end of the first half).

Additionally, you must not be taken in by an argument that the person you sent off had been substituted earlier in the break. As a knowledgeable referee, you will, of course, remember that no substitution is considered complete until the substitute has entered the field of play with your permission (NCAA and NFHS require only beckoning by the referee).

Since the alleged substitute neither received permission to enter the field nor actually entered the field, *no valid substitution has occurred.*

SUBSTITUTIONS

Law 5 states that no one may enter the field without your permission. Obviously, that includes substitutes as part of the substitution process, but the requirement is stated in very general terms. As a practical matter, a substitute would not need your permission to enter the field during the halftime break for such reasons as warming up, practicing shots on goal, passing the ball back and forth, bringing water out to a teammate, congratulating a teammate on a half well-played, and so forth. In other words, the substitute's presence on the field presents no problems since it is not an attempt to be taken as a player prior to the start of the second half.

That complicates somewhat the process of conducting a valid substitution during the halftime break. We know what the field has to look like for each team before whistling for the kick-off to start the second half — up to 11 players, all of whom either were on the field at the end of the first half or been given permission by the referee to enter the field as the last step in an official substitution process.

If we were to follow the established protocol, we would only allow the players back onto the field at the end of the halftime break who were on the field at the end of the second half. We would then entertain any substitution requests and manage them the same way we would at any other time during the match when it was legal to do so. As with the substitution process itself, however, we generally play fast and loose with that in the interests of "saving time," particularly in youth play, and we accept any new persons on the field at the end of the break as having been properly substituted for.

You should remember that, although that will probably be acceptable in the vast majority of cases, it leaves you vulnerable when something out of the ordinary happens. For example, suppose you start the second half with A15 on the field. Suppose A15 had not been on the field at the end of the first half and had not gone through any official substitution process. Now suppose, two minutes into the second half, A15 punches an opponent and is shown the red card. We would think that A15 is gone (correct) and that A15's team plays down (maybe).

A15's coach might argue that you never expressly gave A15 permission to enter so that, officially, A15 is not a player of record and the team is not required to play down since A15 is "only" a substitute. Of course, none of that would change the fact that A15 is gone and will still be subject to a minimum mandatory one game suspension … but the coach has now taken advantage of your failure to follow proper procedure and, as a result, A15's team has not suffered the penalty it should have.

In short, in the case of youth play, you will save yourself some possible trouble in the future if you take some brief note who was (or was not) on the field at the end of the first half. Second, regardless of whether your match is using strict Law 3 or youth exception substitution rules, you should determine if a team intends to make any substitutions before starting the second half and, if so, require that the team follow the regular process. Take that into account when deciding how soon before the halftime ends you will start calling for the teams to return to the field. Use the halftime break time, not playing time, to run any substitutions.

Technically, if substitute A22 takes the field for the second half without your permission and in place of A10, a player of record from the first half, who remains on the bench, A22 is in danger of committing unsporting behavior (a cautionable offense) and A10 is in a gray area. The problem is that A22 has not actually committed any offense in that case because we have already noted that A22 is not normally required to obtain the referee's permission to enter the field during a halftime break (otherwise A22 would be guilty from the very moment of stepping onto the field). A22's action becomes an offense only once play starts without having gone through a formal substitution of A22 for A10. After all, A22 could at any moment prior to the kick-off whistle sounding request permission for the substitution or could suddenly run off the field, followed by A10 running onto the field, if either one suddenly realizes that the game is about to begin and each is not in the place they should be.

How you handle that is up to your discretion. You could note the incipient violation of the Law, be proactive, remind A22 that no substitution process has occurred, and then conduct the official substitution (rather like reminding a player who has just been substituted and is performing a throw-in restart to "step onto the field" to make the substitution official before restarting play). You could implicitly "recognize" that a substitution has occurred, even though the proper procedure was not followed, and hope that neither A22 nor A10 commits a red card offense. Or you could whistle for the restart, stop play, caution A22, require A10 to return to the field (or have A10's team restart with only ten players), and then restart with an indirect free kick for the opposing team where the ball was when you stopped play (the correct restart for stopping play for a substitute illegally entering the field). Whether A10 could or should be cautioned also is debatable — A10 neither left nor re-entered the field illegally, A10 was off the field "in the normal course of play," and A10 has the right to refuse to come onto the field so long as that does not delay the restart of play (but A10 remains a player of record).

GOALKEEPERS

Goalkeepers are a special issue because a new goalkeeper can appear on the field prior to the start of the second half in one of two ways. You need to know which way it is because the procedures and consequences are different.

Let's say you have called for the teams to return to the field and you notice that A1 is wearing a goalkeeper jersey even though, when the first half ended, A2 was the identified goalkeeper. One possibility is that both A1 and A2 are players of record and that what has happened is that they have swapped places — A1 is now the goalkeeper in place of A2 who is now on the field as a field player. Another possibility is that A1 is not a player of record, the team has substituted A1 for A2, and A2 is actually sitting on the bench.

The second situation is covered by the section above and the fact that it was a substitution for a goalkeeper makes no difference in your options. Go back to the prior section on substitutions and decide what to do.

The first situation comes under the rule in Law 3 that a goalkeeper and a field player switching places without your permission have both committed misconduct (unsporting behavior). You wait for the next stoppage of play before cautioning both A1 and A2 but, in the meantime, only A1 has the special privilege of the goalkeeper to handle the ball within that team's penalty area. Remember that, since the swap occurred at a stoppage (halftime break), the only requirement missed by the players was gaining your permission. Until you actually whistle for the kick-off, there isn't yet a violation because either player could realize their predicament at the last moment and remedy the situation.

You have the same three choices as in the prior section. You could proactively bring the potential violation to the attention of both players and advise them to seek your permission. You could tacitly give permission for the swap by noting the change in jersey, deciding there was no intent to deceive, and simply warning both players about following proper procedure next time (and hope that nothing occurs to challenge this course of action). Finally, you could allow the violation to occur and caution both players at the next stoppage.

And you thought halftime breaks were simple! If the information provided demonstrates nothing else, it is that you must always be aware of what is going on and what your options are when something does "go on." Although you would like to take a breather and talk among yourselves about the first half, you must remain vigilant about the various things that can go wrong even during the halftime break.

TOP TAKEAWAYS

New Referee: Don't let youth referees kick the ball around during halftime. Don't be talking to the neighbors about next weekend's party. There is much to be done at halftime — chiefly, hydration. Be ready for team tactics, positioning, use of cards and need for cards.

Experienced Referee: You already have the games your crewmates are hoping to get, so teach them. Help them see the game through your eyes. Help them understand why you didn't give the second yellow for a technical violation. Explain the two-minute stoppage where you had to deal with the home keeper: what was said, why you gave that restart. Explain why that penalty kick had to be called. Get the next generation ready to replace you and it all starts with halftime and postgame discussions, when everything is fresh in everyone's mind. Also, if you are an instructor and mentor, can you break down a subject (handling, contact with the keeper, offside) as done with halftime in this chapter — going to all the source material and giving a complete description of the problem and several options?

CHAPTER

09

MANAGE PLAYERS AND COACHES

We interact with people every day. It occurs at work, home, school and other social activities. Our success at interaction forms the basis for our relationships. Those relationships and our ability to develop, nurture and build them become the core competency in how we live our lives and relate to others.

It is no accident that we sometimes take relationships for granted. To become skilled or competent at any task, though, takes time, practice and refinement. In learning to manage people, it's important that we learn and master the subtle building blocks that constitute the relationship. It's even more important in games, since the results of inaction can be unfair and unsafe to the participants.

It's easy for assigners, instructors or supervisors to tell us *what* to do when it comes to managing players and coaches on the soccer field, but much more difficult for them to tell us how to do it.

The process of communication has historically been thought of as a sender, a receiver and a transfer of information between them. We now know that communication is much more than that based on the groundbreaking work of Harvard-educated biologist Humberto Maturana in the 1970s.

Maturana's research showed that the structure of the human nervous system encompassed three interrelated domains of human existence. Those three areas include language, emotions and the body's physiology. Maturana demonstrated that language provides a basis for the world to be distinguished, and that led to human coordination and collaboration. Both skills are important in building constructive personal and professional relationships.

Managing players and coaches is not just about "communication" per se but part of a much bigger process of developing a relationship with them. Learn how to build a relationship, fine-tune observation skills and then practice communication skills to be more successful.

MAKE DIRECT EYE CONTACT

In western culture, making eye contact is the first effective step in connecting with another human. You bring your focus and attention to one specific point in time — the behavior and demeanor of a player or coach. The objective is to orchestrate an "attention-getter" in the mind of the player to be managed (listener). That can be done when issuing a card, for example.

For the timid or less-experienced referee who finds it difficult to "look inside the eyes" of a player, look at the tip of the player's nose or forehead. He or she won't know the difference and you can practice making eye contact.

IDENTIFY THE EMOTION OR MOOD

Players and coaches come in all sizes, shapes and personalities. Those personalities are demonstrated by their emotions and moods. Great coaches prepare their players to play under all sorts of adversity. Players on those teams are generally well-disciplined and well-prepared. Their state of being or mood is enthusiastic and ambitious.

However, when things don't go their way — when they are fouled a few times or receive a caution — their mood quickly changes. Angry players quickly lose their ambition or competitive drive and start looking for excuses, looking for others to blame. Without intervention, the player's behavior can easily turn from anger to a mood of frustration, rage, despair or even resignation.

ESTABLISH RAPPORT

You need common ground before any meaningful communication can take place. That alignment or "rapport" between referee and player can be initiated before the game begins. Introduce yourself and your colleagues to players and coaches during the pregame conference. Make direct eye contact, hold your arm out and with a firm arm grip, shake hands with the coach. Look them in the eye as you introduce yourself and the members of your crew.

At some point, you should walk the field to check for unsafe playing conditions and to demonstrate that you have the welfare and safety of the players foremost. Indirectly, those actions lay the groundwork for establishing rapport — you demonstrate, through action, that the referees are concerned about the participants' safety.

CONVEY THE MESSAGE

In no uncertain terms, the message must be conveyed as simply and effectively as possible. It can be verbal or nonverbal, but must be done in a manner that uses a whole-body approach of language, body movement and emotion. Phrases spoken with conviction such as, "I've got it," "You made your point," or "That's enough" are short and to the point. Having a repertoire of short, concise phrases that can be directed at a player in a non-threatening manner enhances your ability to control the game. As you become more competent at conveying messages, those phrases can be communicated nonverbally with a glance or facial look — just as though they had been spoken — but listened to with the same amount of conviction and authority as if they had been spoken.

DECLARE COMPLETION

Conversations between you and a player are over when you declare them to be, not when they naturally end. How many times have you spoken to coaches about their behavior, only to have a coach endlessly continue the conversation so that they can have the last word? So what? If you've effectively made your point, it may be that the coach wants to save face or avoid being shown up in front of his or her players. Recognizing that possibility allows you to still get your point across and lets the coach retain some dignity.

What's important about that step in the communication process is that when a message is conveyed with authority, there can be no doubt that the referee "meant business." Second-guessing leads to self-doubt and lack of confidence and undermines your ability to maintain control.

TIME TO AVOID COMMUNICATION

Sometimes communication with players and coaches should be avoided. It isn't necessary and can do more harm than good.

Injury occurs. When a foul puts an injured player down, call a trainer onto the field. That is not the time to be hanging around. Don't be available as a target for an argument. Move 15-20 yards away or go consult your assistant referees to find out what they saw. There is little you can say to an angry coach that feels you let the player incur an injury.

Halftime. Between each half is a prime time for communication with your fellow officials about how the game has gone and what can be done to improve it. Assistants may have valuable input to share with you, so ask for feedback and give feedback. Don't let coaches, spectators or others interrupt your halftime break. That time to communicate with your referee team is valuable. Keep unavoidable discussions with others brief. Halftime is the time to debrief as a team. Don't let assistants wander

off, play with the game ball or socialize with spectators.

After the game. That is not the time to speak with players or coaches either, unless they come to you as a sporting gesture. Following a game, immediately meet with your fellow officials, conduct any postgame business and leave the field as soon as possible.

Be especially careful of passing through crowds of spectators who may be upset about the loss. Don't say anything. Stay together, pass through them at your own risk, making eye contact with anyone approaching you. Try to determine their intent. If there is an administrator to escort you to your car, take advantage of that amenity. They may be doing that for a good reason.

As game officials, you have nothing to say to spectators, coaches, players or members of the press after the game — especially explanations for your calls.

LISTEN AND ASSESS THE RESULTS

Sometimes, the message delivered to a player isn't really clear — at least as they heard it. Or they sense a lack of conviction or doubt that you will follow up. Expect to be challenged or tested in every game. The feedback you receive from players and coaches will be the easiest way to learn if you're effective or not. It won't take long to determine if the message in plan A worked. Immediately go to plan B, which might take a few minutes to implement. Take different actions or use different words with separate consequences should that unallowable behavior continue. A cautionary note about possible consequences: Don't make idle threats that can't be backed up. Only address actions available to you to control their behavior.

Those steps occur almost simultaneously in the arena of human interaction — yet each has its own individual human component. At the end of that process, a listener (coach or player) should be making (or thinking) the comment: "That referee really means business."

Effectively managing players and coaches involves communicating with them in a way that galvanizes their attention and causes them to respond to you productively. That is good for the game! The ultimate way to manage players is in a way that they don't realize they're being managed.

TOP TAKEAWAYS

New Referee: Just follow the communication road map presented in this chapter. There are a dozen or more tips that you can instantly begin to use in your games. Re-read the article once a month during the season and add something new each time.

Experienced Referee: You've probably used many tools to develop rapport with players over the years. You've probably got a reputation for being hard or soft on players and many coaches and fans will know if you're the approachable type or not. Use the communication techniques presented to alter some of those perceptions — for the better.

CHAPTER

10

HELP IS ON THE LINE

Assistant referee. The terminology changed years ago because expectations of what "linesmen" do evolved beyond simply managing touchline and goalline calls. What prompted the change and what are the expectations of the assistant referee (AR)?

The game is faster, more difficult to manage and players have gotten more sophisticated. Expecting one referee to control the game is unrealistic.

Assistant referees need to be an active part of ensuring the match goes smoothly. The Laws are clear that the assistant referee shall "assist the referee (subject to the referee's decision and supervision) to control the game in accordance with the rules by: ..." In the specifics that follow, an important aspect of the AR's role is not discussed. The rules state specifically that the AR should assist with things the "referee may not have seen" and that the AR should, "give an opinion on any point on which the referee may request." Nowhere is the issue of assisting in game control discussed.

When a game is successfully officiated, the entire referee crew deserves credit.

Similarly, when there are game-control issues, the entire crew may be at fault.

Many clinics discuss the need for the referee to conduct an effective pregame discussion to set the ARs' expectations and talk about effective crew communication. Those discussions tend to focus on rulebook specifics — what to do when you see something the referee misses or how best to communicate information that the referee requests. When the referee crew performs well, even in the most difficult match, that is sufficient.

STRUGGLE

The issue comes when the game is starting to get out of control; when the referee's actions are insufficient for the level or intensity of play. The referee team is faced with a dilemma that underscores the complicated and sometimes contradictory messages. On one hand, ARs are told "the crew is successful or fails as a crew" and on the other hand, ARs are instructed they "need to refrain from becoming over exuberant in flagging calls that interfere with the referee's performance and game flow or game management." To complicate that further, players expect the same response from the referee crew — whether the incident happens in the center circle or right in front of the AR.

Addressing that issue starts in the locker room, but can't end there. In the pregame discussion, the crew must have a "disaster mitigation plan." No one likes discussing subpar performance; however, the crew must address what it will do if one referee is not doing the job. Outline a series of escalating steps that the crew agrees will help the referee or an assistant get back on top of the situation.

As a first step, experienced referees might instruct the ARs to give a subtle signal regarding game control — a "tightened fist" if the ARs think the game needs to be tightened up. Two-way communication is critical: The referee must acknowledge receiving the information — a "thumbs up" or nod of the head. It becomes one more piece of information for the referee deciding on the proper level of control. If both ARs provide that same feedback, it must lead to a tightening up of the match.

GRAY AREAS

If more intervention is needed, the area directly in front of the AR, closer to midfield, is an opportunity to slowly raise the bar. At whatever level the referee has the bar set, there are "gray areas." Use those areas to tighten things up slowly. If that is part of the team's "disaster mitigation plan," the referee should be able to also slowly rein in the game. If that isn't working, slowly expand the area where as an AR you will tighten things up. Never get to the point where it is clear you are doing the referee's job right in front of him or her. That is a critical point because as much as you would like to help control a game to not let it get out of hand, as an assistant, you cannot take the game away from the referee. Try to minimize the field areas where the issues occur. Unless it is a misapplication of a rule, it must be done slowly and cautiously or the referee loses all credibility and the team — the referee and you — will fail. In rare cases in which player safety is an issue and a halftime discussion cannot wait, the assistant might request the referee come for a quick conversation. Say what needs to be said in 10-12 seconds in order to "save the match."

HALFTIME ADJUSTMENT

It's important to be able to recognize when things are not going well in the game at any level. It's a feeling you have to learn over time and with experience. Understanding when to listen to what the players are saying/doing, and how to address it is a big step in an assistant being able to help a referee and develop a great performance. Typically, if the crew's performance is an issue, it began in the first half. Halftime requires a frank and honest discussion about how the crew needs to get control back. The referee should outline very specific actions the crew will take in the first five minutes of the second half. For instance, "We will all tighten it up — call all 50/50 fouls that are not clear advantages." "The ARs will indicate (tightened fist, 'thumbs up,' flattened palm) during the next five minutes." "Whistle tone will be proportionately ratcheted up." Remember that the coaches will also be making halftime adjustments.

Telling the referee everything is going fine when it's obvious that there is a problem does not serve anyone. The referee is not helping when the halftime discussion starts with, "How's it going?" when there is a train wreck occurring. If the referee knows there is an issue, start the discussion with, "How are we going to get this game back?"

No one likes to be involved in a game that gets out of control. No one likes to think about that outcome.

Having a plan to recover from a brewing disaster — developed as part of the pregame and implemented when needed — is a requirement for ensuring the referee crew is successful, even when the referee is not having his or her best game.

TOP TAKEAWAYS

New Referee: Listen carefully to the referee's pregame discussion. If a point is unclear, ask questions. If some aspect of game control isn't covered, ask what the referee would like you to do. Perhaps the most important point, when you are the referee — especially when you are working with senior people on your line — tell them what you want. Be the boss so everything goes according to your plan. Give and get feedback after the game.

Experienced Referee: You've had games "go south" on you and hopefully you analyzed the reasons why. Many of those games are the result of a referee team not working well together, with either too much or too little help coming from the touchlines. Here are a dozen or more techniques you might incorporate into your games and some tips to help you when you run the line for a newer referee. Use your halftimes effectively.

CHAPTER

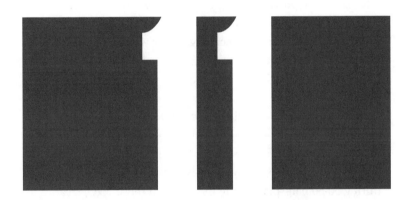

WEIGH GOALKEEPER SAFETY

If a non-referee asks you if officiating soccer is basically applying what's written in the rulebook to a game, how would you answer? Your first thought might be that it seems like most of the rules and their application are at the "discretion of the referee" — the proverbial "gray area." So as straight-faced as possible, you might say, "Yes."

The tough part about officiating soccer well is how to apply the right discretion at the right time. Perhaps no part of the game has more gray area than the goalkeeper's right to protection.

The *Laws of the Game* allows keepers to compete with one powerful, extra tool — the use of their hands, the ability to take the ball away from the feet of the other players. Because of history and tradition, many officials give keepers extra latitude during 50-50 balls played into the area, but those privileges should not render strikers impotent in their quest for a goal. It is the quest to score that's the whole point of the game. It's the keeper/striker "gray area" that gets coaches and fans wound up — and often leaves referees with much indecision.

The gray area of keeper protection often receives little to no attention in any instruction. If anything, it had turned from gray to dark gray. Part of the reason is the fluid nature of the game, plus the uniqueness of the goalkeeper position. Unlike the other 10 opponents, keepers have special rights (use of their hands) inside the penalty area. However, *outside* the penalty area, they have "no more privileges than any other player." Keeper's teammates *think* they have added protection, and thus, that is a strong point of contention.

As referees, safety is our primary concern, one of the three main tenets of the game. Inside the penalty area, that doesn't change. It doesn't change when keepers spend a good amount of time on the ground with their faces near the ball and consequently, opponents' cleats. Outside the penalty area, like anywhere else on the field, if players are on the deck and their safety is in jeopardy, blow the play dead and apply the indirect free kick restart. Do the same inside the penalty area for the goalkeeper. Coaches and fans may complain that you have taken away a goal-scoring opportunity, but the players' safety is always trump. Let that not be misunderstood. There is bound to be contact with the goalkeeper. It is a limited-contact sport and the keeper is the last line of defense before attackers celebrate.

Not every contact between goalkeepers and opponents should be interpreted as a foul by the attacker. Get into the habit of paying closer attention and ask yourself questions such as, "Was he or she knocked out of the way intentionally?" "Did the attacker gain an unfair advantage by making contact with the goalkeeper?" "Was the contact careless enough to require a stoppage?" "Was the keeper's safety put in jeopardy because of the attacker's actions?" Those rule-of-thumb criteria about contact with a goalkeeper may make the decision to stop play or not more obvious.

If those questions cannot be answered in your mind, look to see the results of the play. Sometimes, a slow whistle may save you from many problems with the teams or the coaching staffs. If the ball goes to a defender who clears it or a shot goes over the goalline resulting in a goalkick, you won't have to make that delicate decision of whether or not to stop play. The slow whistle gives you time to think — time to review it in your mind.

Your primary concern is the players' safety, while upholding the *Laws of the Game*. Games result in opportunities for both teams to score and deny goals. You may indeed be put in the less-than-desirable position to decide whether or not to give the goalkeeper more liberty during contact. By Law, keepers maintain the same rights as the other 20 players in contact situations. Also, there are a number of technical violations keepers can commit — holding the ball for more than six seconds, touching it after a throw-in or when kicked deliberately by a teammate.

Make a conscious effort to evaluate that thorny scenario throughout any game. Focusing on players' safety and the game's ultimate purpose, perhaps the "discretion of the referee" can become a consensus. All of a sudden, it's not so gray.

TOP TAKEAWAYS

New Referee: Safety is your primary concern, one of the three main tenets of the game. Follow the guidelines to help you keep the contest safe.

Experienced Referee: Keeper's teammates think they have added protection, and thus, that is a strong point of contention. Your years have shown you the need to keep the players safe, but now you are starting to blend the emotions of those trying to score and those trying to defend. It received little to no attention in instruction. So, if you are mentoring some newer referees, it's a great topic to dissect.

CHAPTER

A TRIFLING ADVANTAGE

It has been said that "trifling" and "advantage" are related in many ways. Certainly the result is the same: no whistle. Many new and not-so-new referees struggle with understanding those two concepts, especially the contrast between them. Let's define the two terms.

1. TRIFLING

"Trifling" derives from a no-longer-included (but still very much in force) International Board Decision following Law 5, which said, in part: "Constant whistling for trifling and doubtful breaches produces bad feeling on the part of the players and spoils the pleasure of spectators."

In short, referees are instructed to only whistle infringements that matter — to not be overly picky about the exact spot of a throw-in or a free kick 70 yards from goal or whether the keeper carries the ball two inches outside the penalty area when punting the ball. Players may be momentarily and ineffectively held, pushed or charged, but that contact may have so little impact on their ability to continue the attack that the referee should do nothing more than silently congratulate the attacker on playing through. Players' development is accelerated when they learn to play through physical contact. No matter what level a player is at, there is always more physical play at the next level — as well as a greater expectation that the referee will allow more.

The concept of a trifling offense is never a reason to ignore nasty play, because it often escalates. A slightly bad tackle, that is also late, may not affect the scoring chance in the next few seconds, but the pain from it will be remembered. That contact may distract the recipient during a similar play 10 minutes later. Referees need to keep track of the giving and receiving of such "gifts," and make sure players are aware that the guilty acts are noted. It's good refereeing to swing by and tell any benefactor that, the moment the contact affects play, the whistle blows. Or, more succinctly, "Don't hold!"

The boundary between what is trifling and a foul that is whistled depends on the demonstrated skill and physical play of the players, the importance of the match and minor factors like slippery footing and poor lighting. Experienced players expect to give and receive more personal attention. Managing contests involving teams that have different expectations of allowable physical play is an advanced skill. The line the referee draws will almost certainly be higher than one team thinks fair, and lower than the other wants.

2. ADVANTAGE

The advantage clause of Law 5 reads: "… Allow play to continue when the team against which an offense was committed will benefit from such an advantage. …" A consequence of that is that advantage is never applied to situations in which no foul has occurred. In a nutshell, the advantage signal announces to all, "I saw that foul, but not stopping play for it." If the foul also merits a caution, the referee can loudly say, "I'll be back for you, number 6." That lets opponents know they need not plan to even the score, because the referee will take care of it. A foul deserving a send-off should only have advantage applied if the offended team is almost certain to score in the next few seconds. Not only does the immediate red card better serve the game, but the send-off is more easily "sold" if there is minimal time lag.

Finding the right psychological moment to announce advantage is another advanced skill. If advantage is signaled too soon, and the advantage dissipates, referees degrade their credibility by stopping play for an offense they said they weren't stopping play for. But it looks silly and self-serving to call, "Advantage!" after the shot has gone past the keeper into the net. Sometimes, especially around the penalty area, righteous advantage calls arrive and depart too quickly for the referee to get to savor them. The match has moved on, and yelling "Advantage!" late only confuses players.

The guideline is to wait no more than two to three seconds to decide whether the advantage remains. There are no silent advantage calls. You may have waited too long, but that's not an excuse to forgo giving the signal — it's just bad timing.

THE DIFFERENCE

Trifling and advantage have exactly one thing in common — the whistle isn't blown. The key tool at your disposal isn't your whistle, but your voice. Talking to the players helps manage both kinds of events. Advantage, of course, includes calling out "Play on!" or "Advantage!"

For situations where players suspect that a whistle is about to be blown (such as non-deliberate ball-to-hand contact), shout something like, "Keep going!" (It is amusing to see the ball short-hop off a player's elbow, followed one-third of a second later by the referee saying, "Keep going!" followed by the parents' shouts of "Handball!") For situations in which players think an offense was committed, but you see it differently, it is useful to shout, "Nothing!" or "Nothing there!" to let everyone know: a) I saw the incident, b) I've decided there was no offense and, c) keep playing. Years ago, some referees called out, "Play!" in those situations. Not only is "Play!" too close to "Play on!" but it's more effective to shout, "Nothing!" because it starts on a lower pitch. That keeps you from sounding overly excited, which helps manage the match tone.

EXPAND YOUR VOCABULARY

Develop your own repertoire of words or phrases to consistently communicate nonoffense and trifling contact. For advantage situations, yell out, "Play on. Advantage!" Make sure players understand when you are saying that you saw no offense (or at most, trifling contact), and when there was an offense, but they need to keep playing anyway. Like an orchestra conductor, it's your job to allow the players to play beautiful soccer, both by eliminating sour notes and letting them know when it sounds fine to you.

TOP TAKEAWAYS

New Referee: Trifling and advantage are tough concepts. Many referees get into their second and third season without fully understanding them. Read this chapter and periodically re-read it to apply the skill-set appropriately.

Experienced Referee: The broader concept of call-sorting (no contact, trifling, advantage, private word, public word, yellow card, "orange card," red card, suspension, termination) needs to be part of your overall knowledge of game management. Within that, a complete understanding of the difference between trifling and advantage is necessary.

CHAPTER

DON'T GET HUNG UP ON CONSISTENCY

Ralph Waldo Emerson was an early 19th Century American social philosopher and essayist. Though he likely knew nothing about soccer as it was developing in England near the end of his life (he died in 1882, some 20 years after the rules of English football were first written down), he had something very relevant to say about refereeing. In a famously quoted 1841 essay titled, "Self-Reliance," he stated, "A foolish consistency is the hobgoblin of little minds. ..."

We hear a lot about consistency from coaches, players, spectators and others. It is almost as highly prized as the Golden Rule. Claiming a referee is inconsistent is thought to be a serious charge. We often hear things like "Call it both ways, ref!" or "You didn't call it down there, ref, so why are you calling it here?" Coaches tell referees they want the same things called the same way no matter when they happen (first 10 minutes versus the last 10 minutes), no matter where they happen (either end of the field or in the middle) and no matter how it is committed (a foul is a foul is a foul).

Frankly, that is nonsense and causes referees more trouble than it solves. Like many things, it has enough truth and utility to make it seem a good thing on the surface. But the appearance becomes deceiving as we look at it closer. The deeper we go in analyzing what consistency would mean on the field, the more we run into Emerson's argument that consistency can become foolish and, when it does, it detracts from our most fundamental objectives as officials.

The most common definition of "consistent" relevant to the issue is "free from variation or contradiction." Applied to referees, it means roughly that our response to situations should be the same when the circumstances are the same. Looked at that way, it seems impossible to argue otherwise. The problem arises when we look at the core of the definition — the assertion that "the circumstances are the same" — because I would argue that circumstances are *never* the same in some potentially essential way.

COMPLEXITY OF FOULS

Think for a moment about the "persistent misconduct" caution. Player A5 carelessly trips B8 five minutes into the match, then carelessly charges B9 two minutes later, and almost immediately afterward deliberately handles the ball. A5 is clearly out of control and should be cautioned for persistently infringing the *Laws of the Game* (either immediately or after an appropriate warning). A5 might argue that the handling offense didn't deserve a caution and was no different from her previous fouls — which weren't cautioned — so we are being inconsistent in cautioning action X but not cautioning actions Y and Z. The answer is twofold: First, the caution was not for the handling but for something entirely different (a pattern of fouls) and, second, the handling offense was not the same as the previous two fouls precisely because it had been preceded by two other fouls.

Or consider B5 elbowing an opponent while competing for the ball. We might stop play for a direct free kick restart, we might apply advantage and allow play to continue or we might do nothing beyond warning B5 about his behavior. Indeed, for the sake of argument, assume that three different players (B5, B12 and B7) elbowed three different opponents in exactly the same way — in other words, the three acts of elbowing were indistinguishable (unlikely, but assume it anyway). What would justify three different responses to those otherwise "equal" fouls?

In the first case (direct free kick restart), the foul occurred 20 yards up from the opponent's goalline. The application of advantage might be appropriate if the foul occurred 20 yards up from the defender's goalline, the fouled player's team retained control of the ball and continued its attack. The warning might be the best decision if both players were elbowing, neither player was showing an adverse reaction or gaining an unfair advantage and were continuing to "play through" the actions.

In other words, a foul is really a complex event that goes well beyond the simple act of pushing, tripping, holding, handling, jumping at, interfering with the goalkeeper's release of the ball into play and so forth. The event includes critical criteria such as when it happened, where it happened, what immediately preceded it, what followed it (i.e., the result), the general tenor of the match, the experience of the players and many other factors. The offense we call "dangerous play" is almost completely dependent on the age and skill level of the players where the specific physical action by the offender is only the starting point.

SEE THE PLAY

What all that boils down to is that there is no specific thing called "consistency" (except in the minds of players, coaches and spectators); there are levels and degrees of consistency. What is far more important than consistency is usefulness.

Decisions about how to handle offenses begin with *seeing* the offense. We cannot respond effectively to what we do not see (where "we" includes all members of the officiating team). So, in a sense, our first task is to see what needs to be seen and that is a function of positioning, which in turn is the result of combining fitness with reading play. Positioning is an art based on probabilities, the purpose of which is to maximize the likelihood that we will be aware of anything that might adversely affect our ability to do our job. We take certain positions or follow positioning guidelines on the theory that doing so will optimize that purpose, but we never know whether our actual position is working until after the fact (it did or it didn't). As a match progresses, we adjust our approach to positioning based on a developing sense of what the teams (and individual players) are doing. That means that, theoretically, we should "see more" of what is important as we gain more information about player behavior and modify our positioning accordingly.

CATEGORIZE THE OFFENSE

Once we see an event, it needs to be categorized. That is often referred to as "call sorting" and involves identifying that event as, at minimum, no offense, a doubtful or trifling offense, an offense to which advantage should be applied or an offense for which play should be stopped. Of those four basic categories, the most important dividing line is between "no offense" and the other three which all presume that the action is an offense. To the extent consistency is needed at that stage, it is in understanding and properly applying the criteria that enable the official to decide if a player's action is an offense of some sort.

The factors that cause an event on the field to be placed in one of the three "offense" categories are numerous, complex, shifting and extend far beyond the simple action of a player. And that is only for fouls! For misconduct, we need to consider more criteria that are even less objective (remember, "intent" is, by and large, not a critical element in a foul but is at the heart of determining misconduct). The decision as to which of those three categories applies expands the concept of consistency to include many factors which players, coaches and spectators seldom see, much less appreciate. All perceptions by anyone other than the officials (or an assessor) are filtered through innate biases that color their view of the event and make suspect their claims for consistency.

Having seen and categorized the event, the final step is to respond to it with some action. For that, complete consistency is necessary. In other words, every event determined to be not an offense should receive exactly the same response by the referee. Every event determined to be an offense for which play should be stopped should be followed by a stoppage of play. For something determined to be a trifling offense, there remain a variety of possible actions — ranging from doing nothing in particular, having a brief private word or engaging in a public admonishment — and the choice among them cannot be held to any consistency standard as the choice must depend on many unquantifiable factors.

ALL THINGS ARE NOT EQUAL

Of course, all other things being equal, consistent is better than inconsistent. However, "all other things" are seldom equal and referees are the only people on the field who are able to know that. Being consistent provides clearer guidelines that players can use to modify their behavior in response to what they see the referee doing, and that is a good thing generally. But, as a match unfolds, its character can change as well and consistent responses early in a match may not be useful under those changed circumstances. The charge to "be consistent" can blind the referee to the need to change for the good of the specific game and become the sort of "foolish consistency" which Emerson said was the "hobgoblin of little minds."

By the way, that phrase in Emerson's day and age meant that it was something that caused fear and distress out of proportion to its importance for those with limited intellect. Sure doesn't sound like referees should fall victim to that problem.

TOP TAKEAWAYS

New Referee: Players, coaches and fans expect consistency. They expect an action that was called a foul in the first five games of the season will be called a foul today. They expect the second time they see you in a season, they know what actions will lead to them getting a misconduct card. Rightfully, they expect what you allowed as trivial contact five minutes ago will go un-whistled if it happens again. This chapter explains the high-order skill-set that you are starting to develop to make tiny adjustments — when doing the right thing for that game is more important than the heralded consistency.

Experienced Referee: You've started to become the concert maestro with the baton firmly in hand. You've made plenty of mistakes in the past decade, but you are starting to see when your decisions have to change to maintain control. You can now sense when to allow the players more latitude (they've proven they can handle it) and when you need to bring things down a notch. Maybe without knowing you are doing it, you have been "call sorting" and not being as consistent as earlier in your career but with better results. To be a truly effective referee, you have got to understand the intricacies.

CHAPTER

STYLES OF PLAY DICTATE REFEREE STYLE

Soccer is about the five senses. Players want a taste of victory, have an eye for the ball, a nose for the goal, hear footsteps and, most importantly, develop a feel for the game.

Referees are taught about the senses, for example, smelling a foul. You shouldn't underestimate how important it is to have a feel for the game. That subject is often stressed at clinics. When a feel for the game is discussed, it is usually in the context of intensity and players' skill level. Instructors discuss where to draw boundaries — foul versus no foul; yellow card versus admonition, etc.

A critical component of "feel for the game" is understanding what might happen next and properly positioning yourself to see what occurs. A feel for the game implies making adjustments. As you sense what is happening, you adjust accordingly.

Different styles or defensive patterns require referees to make adjustments in running patterns and areas of focus. The following thoughts include input from Kim Vieira, Dr. Bob Sumpter, Chico Grajeda and Lou Labbadia, who are experienced referees, assessors, clinicians and assigners.

What adjustments should officials make? All had a similar thesis: "There is no one right answer," "You'll know it when you see it," and, "There is a big intuitive piece to proper positioning" — the same old saws taught in many clinics. A few strategies employed by teams are below, as well as some referee adjustments. If someone on the officiating crew knows the teams' style, discuss it in the pregame conference.

BIG NUMBERS UP

That style of play is typical of attacking soccer with multiple offensive targets. That usually leaves a wide-open midfield and often has very little constricted midfield play. That match requires referees to be very fit, as there will be a lot of vertical ground to cover (goal to goal). It also requires a heightened reliance on the assistants, as the game feels spread out.

Some considerations for the "big numbers up" style of play include not going as deep as you might in a more controlled style — you do not want to miss anything critical during counterattacks. When given the choice, take a more central vantage point versus one closer to the touchline. It might help shorten the distance to the next critical point in the match. Assistants need to recognize that type of game and quickly expand their area of influence to ensure the "long ball" and "off-the-ball" incidents are covered adequately. That type of match is not only the "big numbers up" style of the attacking national teams, but also has the same considerations in the youth "kick-and-run" game.

FLAT-BACK FOUR

A slower, more controlled match, that allows referees to stay much wider and deeper than the "big numbers up" approach is flat-back four. It requires that both assistants put more emphasis on their offside positioning, watching for defenders switching players more frequently, as they defend a "zone." With the assistants (appropriately) more focused on offside, referees should expect less help off the ball and may have to broaden their perspective.

As the game progresses, look for more one-on-one attacking down the touchlines. Later in the match, there is strong potential for frustration to set in as attackers press harder for a goal. That leads to attackers "embellishing" and requires diligence on positioning — to properly evaluate any contact. One should also expect more through-balls and the "wave the arm at the offside" defense. The referee team must be at a heightened alertness level on the close offside situations. Should one of those not-offside decisions result in a goal, referees should expect the defense to challenge the assistant and be ready to lend their presence and conviction to the assistant's decision. Youth games with inexperienced or not fully coordinated offside traps provide similar challenges.

PACKED MIDFIELD

That is a match-control challenge. There will be more people, and hence, more challenges in the midfield. It is important to recognize that early — set limits to minimize frustration and retaliation. Every ball at midfield will be challenged, so that match requires lingering a little longer with the play and not releasing your attention too soon. You want to observe retaliation or after-the-play fouls, likely in that style of game.

Positioning is important. You do not want to interfere with play. Staying wide is a must — to have the appropriate frame of view; however, getting across the midfield has to be timed to not interfere with the play and any potential counterattack. When play allows an equally technical vantage from either side of the field, bench-side is preferred. Should there be a situation in which the benches want to get involved, you will be in better position to prevent that before it happens.

Another aspect to be alert for is the tactical foul to stop the counterattack. In that packed midfield environment, once attackers get through the midfield, they usually have a numerical attacking advantage (four-on-two, etc.). Astute midfielders know that and will try to stop the play before the attack can generate the numerical advantage. That must be dealt with or the attacking team will be frustrated and begin retaliating against its opponents. The youth analogy to that situation is the small, cramped field where there is potential for contact on every ball — U-12 playing on a U-10 field or during tournaments on temporary fields.

SHADOW STRIKER

Look for fouls on players with their backs to the goal. The purpose of those fouls is to intimidate the frontrunner and disrupt the distribution. In that case, be very aware of persistent infringement by one single defender. Also, look for a pattern by the defense; recognize and punish the action. A caution for unsporting conduct may go to a player who has just committed his or her first foul, but is the third or fourth foul on the frontrunner in a short period of time. That system also lends itself to overlapping runs up the wings, as the distributor looks to get the ball out of the crowded center of the field to the open flanks. Referees have to anticipate those overlapping runs, especially on their diagonal. Assistants can help on their side of the field, but often they are busy with critical in/out decisions as the wing lets the ball run toward the goalline before making a centering cross. Nearby defenders make goal kick/corner kick decisions contentious.

TEAM SWITCHING SYSTEMS

Typically, teams may change systems of play after a specific event (goal scored, card, etc.) and referees must recognize when that occurs. When teams move from their preferred system to another one, it is usually due to something that has occurred on the field of which you should be aware. For instance, a key player in the scheme is injured or less effective than hoped. When that happens, there is typically a flurry of "internal" communication among the team — instructions from the technical area or dialogue among the teammates. There might also be a substitution — either someone from the bench or a reassignment of duties. A midfielder becomes a defender, for example. When that occurs, referees should reevaluate the team's approach to the match and readjust their positioning. If possible, convey the new strategy to your assistants during a short stoppage.

SECOND HALF

Begin the second half by reassessing team tactics. What adjustments did the team make at halftime? Do not assume that the second half will begin the way the first half ended. Lapses in concentration during the first few minutes of the second half could be very detrimental to match control and flow.

After a goal, a team might have to move from a packed midfield to an alternative if the team goes down a goal. The team may not switch, so the message is the same: Reevaluate, don't presume before you analyze the situation. However, be prepared to see something different. A team will be more pressed to change systems later in the match rather than earlier. That may be more difficult to figure out, as there may not be a precipitating event (look for substitution patterns). The cues include the urgency with which the team gets the ball back into play and its desire for the referee to get involved in the game's pace ("Hey ref, they are wasting time").

In general, reading the game still often requires a little "I'll know it when I see it" mentality. However, some of the cues or signals might be helpful in ensuring referees are better positioned to assess the incidents that need their evaluation. In all cases, positioning is paramount, proper fitness to be in the right position to officiate is critical and a "feel for the game" is irreplaceable.

TOP TAKEAWAYS

New Referee: During your initial training, you are not taught the tactics or skills in this chapter. To be good at those aspects early in your career, it helps if you were a player. As you progress into your third and fourth season, you'll start to see some of those match-ups forming. Knowing about it ahead of time will help.

Experienced Referee: Some top referees never do read the game very intricately. They muster through on foul recognition, giving the needed cards and generic positioning mentioned in the *Guide to Procedures*. Once you are open to the inner-world of positioning based on what the teams are doing, your skills will rocket to a whole new level. Work with your mentors.

CHAPTER

15

USE YOUR ASSESSMENT

The final turned into the game from hell for the referee. While players contributed significantly to the match's sour tone, the referee brought problems upon himself as well. While his foul recognition was fine, he failed to appropriately deal with cynical misconduct and poor sportsmanship. And he never effectively "set the bar" to ensure that the players understood when an improper challenge rose from a simple foul to manifestly unfair play.

CHALLENGING ASSESSMENT

That type of game really tests an assessor. Comments will be given to help the referee learn and move forward. But will the referee listen to and accept the comments in the spirit they were intended? Or will he reject everything? What should the assessor suggest to help? What is the assessor obliged to say?

It's easy to say, "You screwed up the game; you failed the assessment." But what, if anything, will the referee have learned from a heavy-handed, verbal paddling?

THE ASSESSOR'S JOB

Is the assessor a judge? Jury? Executioner? No, the assessor's job is to mentor. Maybe that is an assessor's greatest strength — knowing how to speak with referees whether they've had a great game or a disaster. Good assessors attempt to address issues without making referees feel as if they are being belittled or browbeaten.

Referees should understand when assessors are not pleased. And certainly they should know when they've utterly failed in their responsibilities (e.g., issuing two cautions to the same player but failing to send off). But assessors should not demean or destroy. Rather, they must reinforce the learning experience.

A National Referee once said: "I was way over my head, and recognized that early in the match. I just didn't have enough experience or tools in my bag. I got reamed by the assessor. I remember saying, 'How can you help me?'

"I needed help, not scolding. Scolding would work if I knew what to do and didn't do it. But in that instance, help was what I needed because I was placed in a game that I wasn't ready for."

The National Referee's story is right on point. When referees have a problematic game, they need help thinking through viable, alternative practices. Assessors must find ways to get referees to figure out more effective means of game management. If assessors can't provide that help, they are not serving the referee's real needs.

Fernando Alvarez, former FIFA referee and member of FIFA's Technical and Referee committees and current State Director of Assessment for California-North, puts it this way: "The *mediocre* assessor tells the referee. The *good* assessor explains. The *superior* assessor demonstrates. But the *great* assessor inspires."

It's all in knowing how to address match officials in a manner that makes them want to learn, despite how awful they feel in the moments after an ugly match. To be an effective assessor you must have (or develop) the ability to get referees to want to hear what you have to say, particularly when they're under stress.

WHAT REFEREES SHOULD SAY TO ASSESSORS

You worked your tail off for 90 minutes and now some guy sitting on a lawn chair is going to tell you what you did wrong. Think about how best to handle the situation when you've been taken out behind the woodshed for a whipping.

Rejecting assessors' comments and saying you disagree, or you think they are wrong won't get you any points. And you won't garner anything positive to take away from the experience. Letting the assessor pound unmercifully until your self-worth is gone also is unlikely to result in a positive learning experience.

Instead, politely and respectfully challenge assessors to call upon their experiences to help raise your awareness and skill set for future games. Ask questions such as: "What alternative positioning would allow me to observe challenges, yet not be in the way?" Or, "If I'm calling all the fouls but the players are not responding, and aggressive play continues, how can I throttle down the intensity?"

Questions framed in that manner tell assessors that you understand, at least in part, and want feedback on the problems you had. It moves assessors out of "whipping" mode and into a more productive information dissemination mode. After all, isn't the whole purpose of the assessment supposed to be for your benefit and growth?

WHAT CAN ASSESSMENTS GIVE REFEREES?

Assessors must remember that all referees have horrible games, and they feel awful about it. Afterward, those referees want to take back this decision or that one. How should referees feel after the assessment? Hopefully, they should feel motivated to learn and benefit from the difficult experience. Unfortunately, in too many instances assessors lay into referees rather than *leading* the referee through positive, thought-provoking learning.

Remember, you learn something from each assessment. Perhaps the lesson sometimes is that a particular assessor didn't have much you could use. Then there will be those assessments where the advice and inspiration last an entire career.

Referees can help by having the right attitude, taking time after the game to formulate questions for the assessor and by listening carefully. Many times an assessor's suggestion will not make any sense to you at that moment. But invariably, at some future date, it will come back to you and help. Other times, the information will not be worth stressing over, so move on.

As a referee you must ask for help, especially after a disappointing game. Tell the assessor where you think you got stuck, and request suggestions on ways to overcome the deficiencies. Ask specifically what strengths you showed that could work to bolster any weaknesses.

You are paying for the privilege of any information the assessor can provide, so take advantage of the opportunity.

TOP TAKEAWAYS

New Referee: It might be a while before you are formally assessed, but you might be mentored or have an observer. Use them as learning experiences, listen to what is being said and if you think the suggestion meets with your skill-set, try incorporating it. Don't be afraid of assessors.

Experienced Referee: Get your head screwed on right as you listen to the advice given to you. With very rare exceptions, the assessor is there to help you. If you hear something that you think might not work for you, ask for alternatives. Great assessors are going to give you a laundry list of the things you did *right*, so you can keep doing them. If you don't get that, ask, "So, what do you think one or two of my strengths are?"

Notes

Notes

Notes

Notes